Je t'aime Colbert –

Happy Birthday 1994

(now PTO to pg. 80)

Neil
x x x

LIFE ISN'T GOOD
IT'S EXCELLENT

David Robilliard, 1980   Photo: Gilbert & George

LIFE ISN'T GOOD
IT'S EXCELLENT
by
DAVID ROBILLIARD

Edition limited to 1500 copies
First published in 1993 by Gilbert & George
© 1993 Estate of David Robilliard
All rights reserved

Produced in Germany by
Uwe Kraus GmbH, Murr/Stuttgart

ISBN 0 9509693 4 6

For Andrew Heard

These 100 poems were selected by
David Robilliard in the year of his death, 1988

CONTENTS

PERCY PISSHEAD

Percy Pisshead
wets the bed
shits his pants
and craves romance
Percy Pisshead
can't see further
than the end of his nose
and vomits on his clothes
Percy Pisshead
can't remember anything
he did or said
the night before
or the night before
or the night before

WE ARE THE INVISIBLE THREADS

I like silver
you like gold
and you wouldn't turn your nose up
at the jewels I hold
you like things made of platinum
but you look a prat in 'em
you wanted a white porsche
and ended up with a white stick

THE MAGIC TAVERN

A smile of knowingness
and willingness
a murmur of murder
a suggestion of theft
cheek of every kind
you'll find them all
sitting and standing
at the magic tavern
they once had an act
of genuine kindness
but everybody turned
a blind eye

STRETCH OUT YOUR ARMS

Dancing in your mind
doesn't stop a budgie from going blind
singing in the street
doesn't stop you eating meat
crying in the bathroom
doesn't make you the top of the classroom
being a bridesmaid
doesn't mean things stay the same
if self-healing doesn't appeal
there's no helping you
going up and down hills
don't make no flatland
flying into space
don't solve the case
there's a giraffe in my class
with a funky ass
there's a lemon in my soul OH NO

GLOBAL CUISINE

It wouldn't be so bad if you were chewing gum when you put my stamps on but the deposits of food you leave between the stamp and the letters make me worry the stamps will come off.

COME ON OR I'LL TAKE TONY

One here one there
soon mounts up to one everywhere
dogs run in packs
the jack comes before the queen
you set my teeth on edge
ragging in the wilderness
let's go to Paris
come on let's go to Paris
don't be mean

I'm waiting for a phone call
to get me out of here
do I make myself loud and clear?
Let's take our chance
this offer isn't phoney
let's go to Paris
come on
or I'll take Tony

I HUNG MY HEAD IN CHAMPAGNE

I can't remember your name
oh it's always the same
nobody to forget
nobody to remember
nobody to blame
I remember the night you came

WHEN THE RAINBOW
TURNS INTO A CHAINSAW

The remix letters
get better and better
a notice is not ice
but it can be even colder
and harder
there's none for you
you can die
and turn blue

I HOPE YOU'VE SOOTHED YOURSELF BY THE TIME YOU READ THIS

How much pain do you need
before inspiration takes the lead
how much comfort do you want
before you want no more

Right now we're not speaking
a silent argument
a disagreement
if silence were golden
we'd both be rich

Get yourself in a car to my place
and don't start jiving with the driver
just get your ass into gear
it's time you were here

If you stay out tonight
there will be no tomorrow night
nothing to hide nothing to lose
I wouldn't like to be in your shoes

But don't let me tighten the screws
on your emotions
or drain your batteries
what's the matter with you
is it me?

SWAN AND CHERRIES

The child wanted to walk
in the opposite direction
to its mother
and started squealing
like a whistling kettle
as it comes to the boil

I DON'T WANT THE NEWS
I WANT THE MUSIC

Let's take a train
before it rains
too many times
on my window
let's have some fun
before the sun goes down
did I say that
did you do this

A champion spitter
grew more and more bitter
when the babysitter
never turned up
and the spit dried up
beat your drum
and wiggle your bum

SO SO WHAT

Just one spec of glitter
on your face
said lots
about your night before

CONCIERGE AND CHIPS

Of course you won't
get rid of crabs by bathing
does a duck complain
when you give it a pond
Quellada is the crabs'
least favourite paste
the codpiece
and the survivor

NOTHING DOING

All the things you give me to do
to keep me from doing nothing
but what I'm best at
is doing nothing

CHARMING

Twinning
winning
or spinning
is your tombstone
grinning at you?

YOU CAN COMPARE ANYTHING TO ANYTHING PARTS I AND II

I
"Oh you're not still going on about how beautiful you were when you were young are you?"
"Bugger off bat's breath"

II
"The characters you assume are about as attractive as a bottle of bat's piss."
"Haven't you got any character of your own at all?"

19. 5. 86

Dreamt the Queen came to lunch
with me at the Market café
and my auntie Winnie came too
she had on a smart costume
I think the Queen had one on too
the table we sat at is not as big in real life
but dreams do Alice in Wonderland things

HOPE SPRINGS ETERNAL

I've got so much to offer
despite the fact
the odds are stacked
sky high against me
even before things went wrong
nobody came along

LET'S YOU AND I GET TOGETHER

Let's all have a pop star each
lots of fun
on a wonderful beach
let's all have a ball
and sit and stare at the wall

You blew yourself out to sea in a bubble
and giggled your way out of trouble
who sat on your knee in Capri?
Who held your arm in Parma?

And who held your hand in Japan?
Open a blank book
and fill it with wild looks
what makes sense to you
don't make sense to me

I want a song where nothing goes wrong
instead of everybody how about you and me
and then what and then who
time is a rap on a par with your life's map

Get yourself dressed and stop being a pest
you can wear my shoes but not my vest
what was that you said about a four poster bed
and the little one said roll over

Together or far apart
Let's make a start
let's meet in the middle
if you've got the solution
this ain't no riddle

CRY WOLF

He pretended to cry and as she came over to him to comfort
him he screamed and coughed and cried and choked with
laughter and shit himself all the way down to his shoes.
He remembered none of this the next day but when he
went round to her flat that night the lights were out and
she wasn't available for all his knocking at her door
so he went back to his bedsit and cried.

FOR OR AGAINST

**Rebelling against yourself
which is worst
rebelling against yourself
or holding yourself back?**

BOYFRIEND OR BEERBELLY?

The thrill of your company
and the touch of your body
makes me feel fulfilled
I know you'd be
the right partner for me
but I know
it's either going to be
somebody else
or nobody

OFFICES OR SUPERMARKET

**Bill and Ben in their pots
and little weed with second class citizenship
and the little house?
– Got knocked down years ago**

QUARANTINE IS NOT A GOOD PLACE FOR THE HUMAN SOUL

Your socks are off and the going's rough
fables and legends and fairy stories
jack and the beanstalk talk and walk
a tall story old bean
open a tin and try some
a rainbow with a pot of gold
all these heavens above
raining acid and the train's late
haven't you got enough on your plate?

A LITTLE GREY MATTER

Sweeping nations congratulations
shouting your name in all the stations
the stay-at-homes at Christmas
are they better than the Smiths or the Jones's
a little grey matter residing over flesh and bones

MILES SMILES AS HE DIALS YOUR NUMBER

Snatches
from now
and memory
with imagination
are turned
into stories
Miles smiles
as he dials
your number

R. I. P.

A hermit emerged from a cave
and said Rip Van Winkle is your slave
you summon him if you want
by reading of him
or seeing films hearing stories
cuckoos don't cross their arms
or extend their charms
to anybody but the food provider
chameleons don't mingle for nothing
so quiet minimum of invention
sleeping hero embraced as a classic

ARMAGGEDON SEASON

Here comes the bomb
we don't like you
and we want you gone
bring the birds and the bees
to their knees
future phantom generations grumble
at their bleak playpen Earth

YOU'VE GOT A DUMMY IN YOUR MOUTH
AND YOUR IMAGINATION IS DRIBBLING

The beerbellies of your imagination
quiver like jelly
as you fill your hot water bottles
what will you do
when the oasis of thought runs dry
stretch marks on a hungry flat tummy
you're mad I want my mummy

PEOPLE ARE ALWAYS INTERESTED IN A GOOD STORY, ESPECIALLY WHEN IT'S THEM GETTING THEIR ROCKS OFF

Superstitions
come and go
and change shape
some drown in time
new ones are born
as long as the sun shines
on the sands of time

CARRY ON DREAMING

I dreamt about you last night. No angels of the bride in this dream.
There was a theatre in a park, with a stage and tables where two other people and you and I were. You suggested we leave together so I put my drink down and walked out, but you did not follow. Instead you continued talking to another of my ex's, which is what you've become in reality, my latest ex.
I started calling you. It was pitch black. I called and called your name 'til my voice started to go hoarse.

Then I was swimming. I remember thinking there was not enough action from my legs – I was too stiff and I needed more practice.
I wonder how this dream would have concluded if I hadn't woken up. One wonders this many times. Perhaps dreams have no conclusions – hollow like a tube. I've had the running urgency in dreams many times, often escaping, sometimes chasing, like with chasing after you last night

AS OLD AS THE CHESTNUT TREE

Shakespeare joins Jupiter
as an eternal classic
the birds and bees
buzz and sing with glee
'till you make them extinct
or cut down their tree

SAY HELLO

Here comes the jamboree
I don't want tambourines or tea
I want you
I could tell the world your name
but what's the point
I found out after a few weeks of fancying you
I've got the feeling you like me quite a bit too
you don't seem to have changed your mind
of course with a lot of people
the second they've got you they want someone else
but getting that far well,
I'd be prepared to take a jet to get to you
there's just something about you
the things we could do together
is better than any treasure on Earth
You are the person I always hope will be there
your face is a challenge
adoration or disdain
who cares it's just a game
and the only people without a heart are dead
X walked in
not X as in anonymous
just X – get someone else to say goodbye for you
but that's life for you
affairs of the heart are as pink as a fart
I wonder if you're the ace of tarts
you've certainly got character
I hope just a little more finding out
doesn't leave me disillusioned over you
I wish you had the guts to approach me

NO TIME FOR MACROCOSM

Don't shit your guts out
get your nuts out
and the self-appointed
high and mighty
attack their own
sexuality
ha ha
no microscope
just microcosm

EMOTIONAL OVERDRAUGHTS

Shut the door
and put the lights out
the cat's been fitter
since it shed its litter
you're not dead yet
don't be so bitter
armchair psychologists
and personal frames of reference
codes of honour
bullshitters and prima donnas

Codes of honour
and chips on shoulders
with whips and boulders
you don't have to be a musician
to want to rock the world

HUMAN NATURE

I'm never going to speak to you again
and in the same breath "Can I borrow your pen?"

YOU DON'T HAVE TO BE A
BARTENDER TO BE BEHIND BARS

I don't suppose you're interested in whether your life
makes sense to you. You just do what you do, a straight-
forward mammal urge in the human zoo.

YOU CAN CRY WITH LAUGHTER BUT YOU CAN'T LAUGH WITH CRYING

I was in the bath
and I had to laugh
then you said goodbye
and I had to cry

WHERE WE GOING NOW DAD?

**Dad will you buy me a £5 voucher for Woolworths?
Weeeeeeeeeeeeeeeeeeeeeeeeeeeeeeeeeeeeeeeeeeeeeeeeee**

ARE YOU POKER-FACED?

The streamers in my party poppers
landed on your head
you looked funny
with a touch of the Boy George
you didn't like it
but you didn't get ugly over it
I just pointed it in your general direction
I didn't realise what a direct hit I'd score
I was a bit nervous
and definitely embarrassed
and certainly thrilled
'course there are times
when you've got
to play your cards right

WE ENTERED THE BUILDING THROUGH EVERY ORIFICE. IT WAS NEW YEAR AND WE WANTED TO PARTY

Creatures out for the night
hungry for a bite
of each other's light
the words are brilliant
the music is fast
and moving like you
no such thing
as no can do

DO YOU PUT YOUR GEL ON WITH A GUN?

**Do you hear babies scream
as you rub your hands with cream?**

DON'T FORGET TO PULL THE CHAIN

His name is Rick
and he knows every trick
in the book
how to be crazy
lazy
sane
hazy
you name it
he's no daisy

THE PLOT SO FAR

The hero has been threatened
and I've been through a sweaty atmosphere
tonight
choking on smoke – yeuk!
And the hero is far from here
oh dear
oh well
I'll see him tomorrow

SAVED BY THE BELL

"Oh you know her dear, a couple of double entendres, a bit of irony."
"I know, it's like a piss-artist trying to give speech therapy."
"She's coming this way."
"Ladies and gentlemen – time please."
"Quick, let's leave."

ENOUGH TO MAKE HER EGGS GO GREY

Myrtle the Turtle
hurtled through space
determined this time
not to end up
with egg on her face
you can imagine her dismay
when she realised
she was headed
the wrong way

200 LETTERS THE LAST GLASS OF WINE AND NO REPLIES

Five continents
including diamonds
and dinosaurs' bones
nappies and cold sores
everything and everybody
you and yours
all names
from yours to Jones
no names
no games
all game
no fun
all fun
storms and sun
here we go
Geronimo

A TOUCHING TALE

Here come the fabulists
who the hell let you in
has the cat got your tongue
or is it just the way you're standing?
Yes you fucking bastard
wake up!

ELIZABETH TAYLOR

I said hello
to Elizabeth Taylor
and she said
push off
I don't need you
I've got a sailor
and a soldier
and a tinker
and a tailor

NO EXPERIENCE NECESSARY

Now that I'm old
I'm ignored
and have to do
what I'm told
my last years
days moments
poured out of a carton
treated like a cartoon
and the sad thing is
the people doing it to me
don't want to consider
it's their turn next

DAILY NEWS

First light crawls through the window
answers to the name of dawn
the night gallops away with its mares

DOUBLING UP

I thought you were having a Batman and Robin relationship but I realise now it's more like Laurel and Hardy

I'D WRITE YOUR NAME IN THE STARS
IF I COULD

You are my elixir of life
beyond the shadow of a shout
I'd like to fill all five continents with my feeling for you
and I will do space libraries too
I'd tell all the animals in the wild
and in the zoos too if I could
carve your name on every piece of wood
fill the moon with tunes about you
tell the oceans and seas not to tease
and to tell all the fish to grant your every wish
in case you haven't guessed
I'm rather fond of you

YOU CAN LEAD A HORSE TO WATER BUT YOU CAN'T TEACH AN OLD DOG NEW TRICKS

I met a men in the can
who said he was my gran
but I didn't believe or relieve
the little step-dog's toothbrush
"You're not my god-mother-father-son-daughter" I said
"You oughta find somebody else to sing your ditties to
I wouldn't whistle on your bristle
even if it meant I had to miss the last train."

METAMORPHOSIS OF DREAMS

For normal hair
weak plot
sensory overload
dodder dodder
dodder ad infinitum
cryptic and surreal
can you peel a squeal

CHIPS ARE WRAPPED IN PLAIN PAPER THESE DAYS

A bisexual bag of chips
spat out the pips
and got to grips
with the newspaper

PROGRESS

Renty twenty
dirty thirty
warty forty

BANANAPPEAL

I like bananas
because they have no bones
I like the peel
because it stops other people
fingering in my food

A GAZELLE SPRUNG OUT OF A WISHING WELL

You are my obsession
but I'm not your possession
in the procession of my delights
I've really taken the bite for you
my feet are cold
and as I've repeatedly told you
I want to hold you
I'm in love with you

THE TRUTH HOLE

Fighting and backbiting
and writing twisted lies
give us a break
history takes wedding cakes
double takes fakes opaques
and anything you can think of
and after a wink of sleep
the people of the future
will put on their shoes
and march through the sands of time
forgotten thoughts toeing the line

A LITTLE POEM FOR ANDREW HEARD

You don't very often see a goat on a London bus
and if you did there'd be a lot of fuss

GET LOST

I knew what you meant when you said you'd like
to give me a space ship with an allotment.

IT TAKES ALL SORTS

"Oh you're the documentary type aren't you dear –
I'm the sloshy sloppy type myself"
"have you always been a dick 'ead?"
"no only since I've known you"
"don't say yes don't say no don't say I don't know – just fuck off"
"that's an offer I can't refuse"
"your shoes are filthy"
"you've got your head in the clouds as usual"
"you really take the biscuit"
"yeah well you've taken the last of the coffee
and I bought the last lot so you can bloody well go out
and buy some more right now"
"sure sugar"
"ha ha ha – get out of here goat's milk"
"you've got the IQ of a post-diarrhoea chamber-pot"
"that's alright you can handle anything"
"I've got to hand it to you, you're really boring"
"oh well it takes all sorts"
"sounds like you"

CONTINUING IN THE SAME VEIN

"What ails you – is it because you're a failure?"
"Yes that's exactly it. It makes me miserable and
moody
and people who don't want to score bore me
and almost all the ones that do are horrific anyway."
"What are you going to do about it?"

NO HOPER

**You're about as useful as a draught excluder
in a tin in a draughty winter with no tin opener**

OLD FLAMES

I used to know a boy called Rose
who had flames coming out of his nose
which reached right down to his toes
it just shows you
it's never the same
with an old flame
'cause I've never seen him again

YOU THINK YOU'RE GOD

Looking at things
from all angles
you decided
to make a triangle
out of a quad
and the power
of your imagination
will suggest
all the other permutations
but what always
makes you think
you're God?

IF THE TITLE FISHING IN MERCURY DOESN'T MAKE SENSE TO YOU WHAT DOES?

Barbara Stanwyck Moby Dick
and an old
let alone a new card trick
are not just foreign
but alien to people
who you wouldn't get credit with
cards or not
some people plant borders with flowers
others with tanks
I'm going fishing in Mercury

CHARMED WOODS

Go gingerly with the bread man
– there's not much to spare
but there's always room at the fable for you
and if you go out into the woods
the next thing you know
the trees are turned into books full of fantasy

A SILENT PHONE A BROKEN HEART AND HUMAN NATURE

You said you'd give me a ring
how I whistled and sung
and then cried
when I realised it wasn't on
but I punished you in the end
'cause I got off with your best friend

MINOR TOURS

Slip us a fiver
he said secreting saliva
you had a long kipper didn't you
herrings on the bone for you
who me
not for all the sea in China
backlash frontlash
gods and dogs
mirrors mirages
and famine trees
an armadillo on a pillow
a pussy on a willow
what d'you want?

MATINEES DON'T ALWAYS FILL EMPTY DAYS

I've driven my wonderful friend away from our sad little nest
I wonder if we tapped our potential it would be less unhappy
or maybe two new nests
oh the unthinkable
– the honesty to make the break
I loved you
and I'm still fond of you doesn't really do

IT'S A LONG STORY USUALLY MEANS MIND YOUR OWN BUSINESS

"I notice you haven't lit any lately"
"Yes well it's a long story"

WHAT CAN WE DO? THIS THING'S BIGGER THAN ME AND YOU

Who gives a screw
when everyone's dead
a bed of stars
shone over our blank faux pas'
me and my mates
were picketing the gates of heaven
when we fell into hell
and couldn't avoid the smell
of deep fried soul
the devils punched bowels
giving out those fabled therapeutic growls
and smells
blame him for your neurosis
good and bad both male
but capital and small 'h' 's respectively
very neat and tidy
and wages on friday

A MURDERER'S SENSE OF JUSTICE

The twigs
under your foot
crackled
as they cackled
you're next
this isn't surreal
and isn't how murderers feel

A NIGHTMARE AT THE HUMAN ZOO

I was invited to a private view
in the house of reptiles
where there were toadies and snakes
and rats and things
that snap not fingers
but alligators and crocodiles
all grimaces and few smiles
all hungry and poison
as was their wont
and the artist?
He was dead

HOPE FOR THE FUTURE OR NEXT PLEASE

When we become antiquities
and the new lot are on their knees
we remain silently in the breeze
as the person in the hospital says
there's no room for you
– next please

PANIC STRUCK

Nothing could bring security
not the ultimate orgasm
or all home comforts
what's the difference
between an artistic poetic death
and a run-of-the-mill death?

HUMAN DINOSAURS

There you go
drenched in verse
tombola of mothballs
in your purse
cuckoo cultures
descend like vultures
but everyone really knows
it's only a question of time
before each and everyone
is blown away

THIS IS FOR SOMEONE VERY SPECIAL TO ME

I wonder if you can guess
this is for you
forget the corn
about nobody else will do
stormy relationships come and go
but you're special
'cause I said so
grunt and gasp and groan
but no, sitting home alone
to you darling I dedicate this poem

TRUE LOVE

The things you said at the end
were definitely a case of sweet turning to sour
I hope you're happy now with your new lover
I didn't mean to lead you up the garden path
but when my long-standing affair returned from
abroad
I'm afraid once again I went overboard
the only person who secures my heart
for all time
is my old love
the flame may flicker it may roar
but as I said my heart is secured
with the one I adore

REACH FOR THE BLEACH

I've switched the fire off
and got in bed with this book
the music on the radio in the background
I'd be happy to find one of the songs were mine
maybe some other time
excuse me I'm just going for a piss
– back again
everyone wants to feather their nest with the best
what's in it for me?
You must agree with me
the sun don't shine
unless the rainbow's mine
some novels shovel the shit
others talk of fuck and tit
and everyone fights for morals and rights
write to your M. P.
tell 'em about your ecstasy
the D. J.'s cool
switch on the air conditioning you fool
a nature ramble gambles with the weather
if it's hell for leather what's heaven for?

THE BRAIN IS THE ORGAN THAT CREATES THE MUSIC

It's up to the minute and really rather trendy
it's translated in every possible way
you give up the ghost and lose the haunted look
you've given me a lot of pleasure with your book
it's a pity I never read it
I've got so much time on my hands
but I'm out for fun without getting swollen glands
you and me harmony on my knee
spreadeagled on the sands
the sea washes over all those one-night-stands
and in the bottom of the bucket
of the oceans of this world
the ancestors of humanity and dinosaurs
have very deep thoughts

WRITTEN TO AMUSE X

GET OUT GET OUT GET OUT
Oh there's nobody there
COME IN COME IN COME IN
would you like to entourage my partnership?
Let's all go for a dip
and then have a kip in the sun
oh come on, now's the time to have fun
a roomful of friends with nothing to do
you've got to be joking
I said to nobody particular
in this empty room
"have some more"
and they said "are you sure?"
If every shot scored a bullseye
wouldn't life be a bore
you made me feel disgusting,
you'll pay for that
oh please come back I didn't mean it
oh no don't go away
I've got lots of wonderful friends here
and they want you to stay

NO NEWS NO REVIEWS AND NO SENSE OF SMELL

As subtle as
a bottle of bleach
humanity thinks
if it washes
and winks
and blinks
it no longer
stinks

ONE-UPMANSHIP

He was weak and skinny and wore glasses,
with even less interest than talent in sport,
but the one thing he had above the other boys
who were trained as total slaves to butch
consciousness – a fucking big fat dick.

PEOPLE ARE LIKE IVY

I used to wonder
what life was about
now I just wander about
falling onto your lap
should have been romantic
but I couldn't get my
piles off your big toe

MY IDEAL SEXUAL EXPERIENCE

After experiencing Miss Piggy in a beigel
I would move on to Michael Jackson's chimpanzee
then I would have a threesome with an elephant and a flea
then I would accommodate a double-dong all by myself
then I would piss up a spider's ass
moving on to conducting an orchestra of fuckfarts
then I would try to seduce some celibate virgin cycle saddles
(I'm not daft)
then I would play Toad-in-the-hole with Kermy the Frog
then I would be a gigolo in a deprived area
then I would try and make some raunchy clothes out of a pumpkin
(needless to say the seeds would make a necklace)
and the penultimate – more Miss Piggy and more beigel

I KNOW WHEN I'M LICKED

You know when you're beaten
something the cakeshop can't sweeten
take it easy
that's no problem
ride 'im cowboy

YOU ARE WHAT YOU DRINK

In the winter you use more hot water
and in the summer cold
and by the way
you need a shave Dave
and then also you are what you smoke
the pills and powders that you take
the lead and air and everything you breathe
can you isolate your problems
what would you like to drink?

NOT CLOSE ENOUGH TO KNOW
ABOUT THE BAD BREATH

She takes in a bit of culture
in her spare time
he spends his drinking wine
they share a table
but are unable to share
much else

GIVE THEM GRACE AND CALL THEM NATIONS

When somebody you're not sure about
tells you you're full of shit
on a saturday night
then you must take into account
the next day
would be very gay
without their company
sunday night to monday morning:
this is life and it comes without warning
everybody's nobody
the observer's shoe keeps wearing thin
but an old pair of shoes
is easier to get rid of
than a double chin
or a starvation situation

QUESTIONS AND ANSWERS

If someone farts on your martyr complex
do you get vexed?

If you thought you'd lost your good luck coin
through a crack in the floorboards
would you make a thorough search
for it or hope it would eventually turn up?

Do you wear sunglasses so you can stare
at people's crutches and get away with it?

– Answers on a postcard please.

LET ME EAT YOU

I beseech you –
let me eat you
have all you see
on the road to ecstasy
a begging letter to the world
bring your pedigree
to tea

CATGUT YOUR TONGUE

4.15 am.or is it pm.
am I becoming an old queen
never has-been
don't raise your eyebrows at me
or even think of palimony
because I've always been lazy
and I'm stoney broke
so don't choke on those hairs
bristling through the holes in your string vest
what happened?
You were just sweet
then your tongue burst into flames

HEALTHY VEGETABLES

A fly loves
a turd to sit on
people hate them usually
and a dog will eat
your baby's donation anytime
potty isn't it?

I SAY I SAY I SAY I SAY

You didn't have to go to university
to discover you weren't always
the centre of the universe
in fact, that time
you were with those two people
who wanted to make hay
you were definitely in the way

OUTBREAKS OF S & M

Fuck frenzy
always taboo
cowardly killers
on the loose
what's new?
Don't touch each other
everybody wants
to put a noose
round someone else's neck
stock piles of love
stock piles of hate
masturbate
hate
enjoy
destroy

NODDY'S COMEBACK

Noddy lies naked
and crying in the dark
dumped in the PARK OF MORALS
where the thistles whistle
and wolves howl at the moon

RED INK

That's final Lionel
Jean Jacques
wants his money back
Dino doesn't want to know
– does it show?
Kevin thinks he's in heaven
Jean-Paul Pseudonym
the scarlet pimpernel
with a pen.